THE PRAYING ATHLETE™
QUOTE BOOK

VOL 6

PERSONAL
ACCOUNTABILITY

Unless otherwise indicated, Scripture quotations in this book are taken from The Holy Bible, *New International Version®, NIV®*. Copyright © 1973, 1978, 1984, 2011 by Biblica, Inc.™ Used by permission. All rights reserved worldwide.

Published by The Core Media Group, Inc., P.O. Box 2037, Indian Trail, NC 28079.

Cover & Interior Design: Ashlyn Helms

Printed in the United States of America.

VOL 6 PERSONAL ACCOUNTABILITY

We live in a world today
where cameras are
everywhere. The eye in the
sky does not lie. If we taped
our lives for a week and went
back and viewed the film,
what would it say about us?

Accept your limitations in life,
but put people in your life
that can help you overcome
your limitations, so you can
embrace the expectation
without limitation.

Be careful what your eyes see and ears hear. Once we take it in we cannot cast it away— it is always there. Our brain and eyes cannot dismiss what is captured. There is no eraser for the brain.

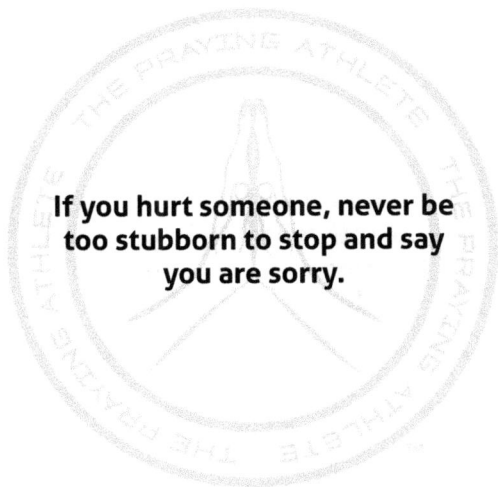

If you hurt someone, never be too stubborn to stop and say you are sorry.

If you were honest with yourself, what could you say to someone? It may open a whole new world for you.

Clients see your sacrifice, work, and availability to help them be successful. Never doubt someone is watching you.

To be aligned with your client means you must be totally committed to what is best for your client, not yourself.

**What does
commitment mean?
I'm with you always.**

**People say, "I love you," but
they never give back to the
person they say they love.
That is not love;
that is selfishness.**

**Do not allow your mind to
overtake your heart.
You heart must win
every time.**

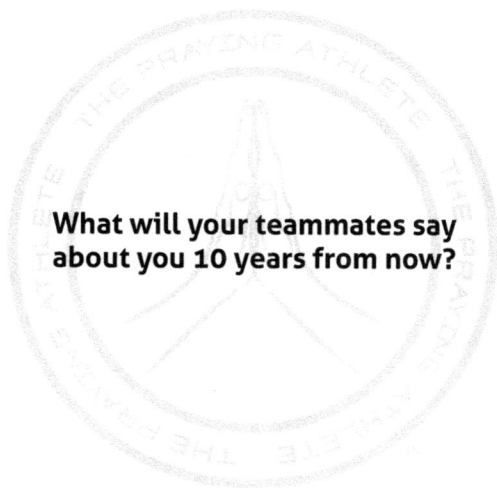

What will your teammates say about you 10 years from now?

What are you reading to help yourself become better at what you do?

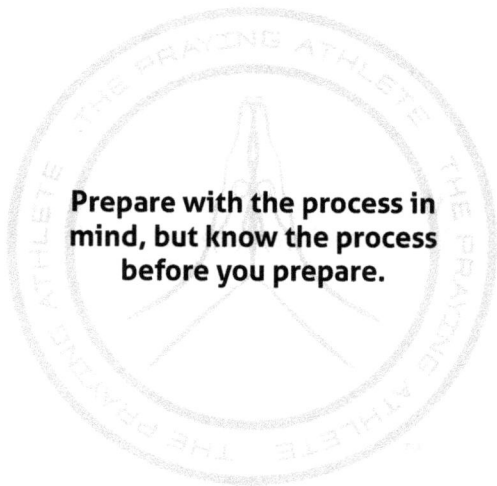

Prepare with the process in mind, but know the process before you prepare.

**Should I say, "what's on TV?"
or "what I should read?"**

I know where I want to go and how I want to get there, I'm just not sure who to take with me, or if they are ready.

Social media robs you of so much. Stay away from it for one week, and watch your life excel in new ways.

When you love someone unconditionally it can be painful, but to put conditions on the love will bring regret.

Not doing something for someone is a tough decision— sometimes it breaks your heart. But, your choice not to may be the new energy they need to do for themselves. This is how you can grow your relationship and make it go deeper and more refined.

Your heart aches for someone
you love when you know you
cannot fix what ails them.
They have to choose to fix
themselves; that cannot be
your job. If you try, it will only
strain the relationship.

Choices can be simple in life.
The right choice, however,
requires diligence and
personal commitment to
finding the right ingredients
for that choice.

I wonder how many people have said, "If I never took that step, what could I have become?" No need to wonder; the answer is millions and millions. People will tempt you with one drink, one smoke of weed, one snort of cocaine or whatever it maybe. They will say things like, "this will never hurt anybody," or "go ahead, try it, have some fun and hang out." Choose today not to be a statistic, but to make choices that will help you standout and not put your life on standby.

A coach cannot fix what you fake. It is time to make yourself better, finish the race, embrace the process, complete the task. Now, ask the coach to shape you and mold you into the athlete he believes you can be. When you humble yourself and ask for help, the growth you truly desire will begin to flow into your life and skill set.

If someone implanted you
with a GPS unbeknown to you
and they were able to track
you, what would they find out
about you that they do not
know today?

**You can control your choices.
No need to derail your life
and career with poor choices.
Make smart choices.**

Why does laziness keep you
from achieving success?
Maybe you need to first define
laziness. One definition of
laziness is to steal away time
and energy from things that
can produce success into
one's life. Internet, TV, social
media, and over-sleeping can
cause laziness.
What are your four?

Think about something in your life. Now ask yourself, will this one thing help guide me to my goals and plans? If so, embrace it with the upmost energy. If not, cut it off and let it fly far far away.

You can build all types of
items with Legos. The Lego
pattern, if followed, can build
some incredible things.
Think about what
the patterns are in your life
and will the current patterns
help you achieve your dreams.
If not, start some
new patterns.

Life sometimes can seem very lonely, dark and feel as though you are the only one battling life's challenges and the curves during the journey. Always look for the signs along the way to tell you what may be ahead. It will prevent you from crashing.

You can control your LEGACY, CHOICES, and JOURNEY with the people you allow to be a part of your story.

May God use my hands and
feet today to captivate an eye
or an ear. May that eye and
ear hear the talent that could
only be God-given. May they
begin to know God through
my life, and may God use this
talent to begin a journey for
those who do not know the
God of the Bible.

THOUGHTS & REFLECTIONS

_____
_____
_____
_____
_____
_____
_____
_____
_____
_____
_____
_____
_____
_____

_____

_____

_____

_____

_____

_____

_____

_____

_____

_____

_____

_____

_____

_____

_____

_____

_____

_____

_____

_____

_____

_____

_____

_____

_____

_____

_____

_____

_____

_____

_____

_____

_____

_____

_____

MY QUOTES

_____
_____
_____
_____
_____
_____
_____
_____
_____
_____
_____
_____
_____
_____

_____

_____

_____

_____

_____

_____

_____

_____

_____

_____

_____

_____

_____

_____

_____

_____

ACKNOWLEDGEMENTS

I want to acknowledge and say thank you to all those that
helped with this project:

Nadia Guy
Ashlyn Helms
My Mom & Dad

All of my NFL Clients, current and former, that have
encouraged me to share these words with others.

ABOUT
TPA

The Praying Athlete is a movement that creates an organic culture of prayer through an uplifting community and authentic conversation.

For more information, visit our website **www.theprayingathlete.com**.

Follow us on social media.

@ThePrayingAthlete

@Praying_Athlete

@ThePrayingAthlete

COLLECT ALL
8 VOL.

Our first volume of *The Praying Athlete Quote Book* addresses the topic of playing the game. Quotes and thoughts from Robert B. Walker, paired with Scripture from God's Word, allow readers to get a good idea about what playing a good game looks like.

Our second volume of *The Praying Athlete Quote Book* addresses the topic of teamwork. Quotes and thoughts from Robert B. Walker, paired with Scripture from God's Word, allow readers to understand what it means to be a good teammate and surround yourself with people who lift you up.

Our third volume of *The Praying Athlete Quote Book* addresses the topic of growth & preparation for the future. Quotes and thoughts from Robert B. Walker, paired with Scripture from God's Word, allow readers to know that even though the future is uncertain, there is a plan and purpose for everyone.

Our fourth volume of *The Praying Athlete Quote Book* addresses the topic of keeping the right mentality. Quotes and thoughts from Robert B. Walker allow readers to understand how staying in the right mindset can improve overall performance.

Our fifth volume of *The Praying Athlete Quote Book* addresses the topic of staying motivated. Quotes and thoughts from Robert B. Walker allow readers to become motivated to accomplish their goals, even when they feel they are not up to the task.

Our sixth volume of *The Praying Athlete Quote Book* addresses the topic of personal accountability. Quotes and thoughts from Robert B. Walker allow readers to think about how they can better themselves. Whether its ending a bad habit or saying no to anything that may hurt themselves or others, staying accountable will benefit one's character and performance.

Our seventh volume of *The Praying Athlete Quote Book* addresses the topic of living life. This volume is the first part in a two part living life series. Quotes and thoughts from Robert B. Walker give readers a better understanding of how to live life to the fullest.

Our eighth volume of *The Praying Athlete Quote Book* addresses the topic of living life. This volume is the second part in a two part living life series. Quotes and thoughts from Robert B. Walker give readers a better understanding of how to live life to the fullest.

CHECK OUT OUR

THE PRAYING ATHLETE™
PHOTOGRAPHY
QUOTE BOOKS

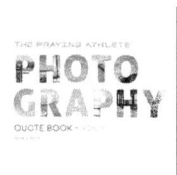

VOL. 1

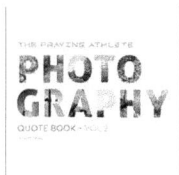

VOL. 2

VOL. 3

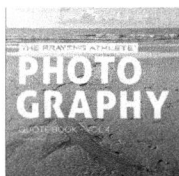

VOL. 4

*The Praying Athlete Photography Quote Book*s celebrate God's glory and magnificence through His creation. They contain photos taken by Robert B. Walker, paired with his words of wisdom, motivation, and inspiration.

FOR MORE INFO AND MERCHANDISE, PLEASE VISIT
WWW.THEPRAYINGATHLETE.COM

www.ingramcontent.com/pod-product-compliance
Lightning Source LLC
Chambersburg PA
CBHW071746020426
42331CB00008B/2197